The Book Lover's Companion

Personal Reading Log,
Book Review Prompted Journal,
& Book Club Guide

Melissa Pennel

Melissa Pennel / Follow Your Fire Publishing
FollowYourFireCoaching.com
Sacramento, CA.

Ordering Information:
Quantity sales: Special discounts are available on quantity purchases by corporations, associations, and others. For details, contact the publisher at the address above.

The Book Lover's Companion: Personal Reading Log, Book Review Prompted Journal, and Book Club Guide— 1st ed.

Paperback isbn 978-1-956446-07-4
Hardcover isbn 978-1-956446-08-1

THIS JOURNAL BELONGS TO

_____

If found please contact at:

_____

MORE JOURNALS BY
THE AUTHOR

The Questions You'll Wish You Asked: A Time Capsule Journal Series

A Time Capsule Journal for Mothers & Daughters

A Time Capsule Journal for Mothers & Sons

A Time Capsule Journal for Fathers & Daughters

A Time Capsule Journal for Fathers & Sons

A Time Capsule Journal for Parents & Children

A Time Capsule Journal for Grandfathers

A Time Capsule Journal for Grandmothers

A Time Capsule Journal for Grandparents

The Questions You'll Wish You Asked is a journaling book series consisting of prompts to capture stories, memories, and wisdom from parents and grandparents of all ages and stages.

Are you asking the questions you'll wish you had?

Learn more at FollowYourFireCoaching.com

GUIDE TO THE BOOK LOVER'S COMPANION

This journal is dedicated to Tamara,
who always reminded me to do the "flips and twirls" while reading.

INTRODUCTION

Hello, dear reader.

The journal you're holding will guide you on a unique book journey that you chart yourself.

It begins with space to fill in your own reading table of contents, so that you can easily reference the books you've read. That section is followed by over one hundred pages to review the next sixty five books you read. Each review space includes not just ample room to write, but prompts to get you thinking and unstuck from the overwhelm that a blank page can sometimes cause.

Following this is a book club discussion guide, which will provide a handy jumping off point for any conversation you may have about a book with other people. Next, you'll find a section to track your "to read" list, so that you can more easily keep track of books you encounter but don't yet have the bandwidth for. There's also a section for books lent and borrowed so that you never accidentally steal a book (and get to pester whomever accidentally steals yours for all eternity.)

Finally, you'll find a section for books you want to recommend and to whom, because the only thing better than reading an amazing book is getting someone else in your life to follow suit. The journal concludes with the Reading Habits Calendar, a place to track your books read in a year.

This is a journal but it's also a reading love story: a testament to the unique relationship we all have with each book we read. If you appreciate this journal, please consider writing it a review online, suggesting it to your book club, or gifting it to another book lover in your life.

Books make us think, feel, and look at the world differently. Taking a moment to write about how and why can create a meaningful record of not just books read, but life lived.

I'm so glad you're here.

Sending love, a hot cup of coffee, and the comfort of a cozy nook with good lighting,
Melissa Pennel

READING TABLE
OF CONTENTS

Book Title	Classic	Historical Fiction	Crime/Horror	Romance	Fantasy/Sci-Fi	Contemporary Fiction	Non-Fiction/Biography			Page number	My Rating
											☆☆☆☆☆
											☆☆☆☆☆
											☆☆☆☆☆
											☆☆☆☆☆
											☆☆☆☆☆
											☆☆☆☆☆
											☆☆☆☆☆
											☆☆☆☆☆
											☆☆☆☆☆
											☆☆☆☆☆

Book Title	Classic	Historical Fiction	Crime/Horror	Romance	Fantasy/Sci-Fi	Contemporary Fiction	Non-Fiction/Biography			Page number	My Rating
											☆☆☆☆☆
											☆☆☆☆☆
											☆☆☆☆☆
											☆☆☆☆☆
											☆☆☆☆☆
											☆☆☆☆☆
											☆☆☆☆☆
											☆☆☆☆☆
											☆☆☆☆☆
											☆☆☆☆☆

Book Title	Classic	Historical Fiction	Crime/Horror	Romance	Fantasy/Sci-Fi	Contemporary Fiction	Non-Fiction/Biography				Page number	My Rating
												☆☆☆☆☆
												☆☆☆☆☆
												☆☆☆☆☆
												☆☆☆☆☆
												☆☆☆☆☆
												☆☆☆☆☆
												☆☆☆☆☆
												☆☆☆☆☆
												☆☆☆☆☆
												☆☆☆☆☆

Book Title	Classic	Historical Fiction	Crime/Horror	Romance	Fantasy/Sci-Fi	Contemporary Fiction	Non-Fiction/Biography		Page number	My Rating
										☆☆☆☆☆
										☆☆☆☆☆
										☆☆☆☆☆
										☆☆☆☆☆
										☆☆☆☆☆
										☆☆☆☆☆
										☆☆☆☆☆
										☆☆☆☆☆
										☆☆☆☆☆
										☆☆☆☆☆

Book Title	Classic	Historical Fiction	Crime/Horror	Romance	Fantasy/Sci-Fi	Contemporary Fiction	Non-Fiction/Biography			Page number	My Rating
											☆☆☆☆☆
											☆☆☆☆☆
											☆☆☆☆☆
											☆☆☆☆☆
											☆☆☆☆☆
											☆☆☆☆☆
											☆☆☆☆☆
											☆☆☆☆☆
											☆☆☆☆☆
											☆☆☆☆☆

Book Title	Classic	Historical Fiction	Crime/Horror	Romance	Fantasy/Sci-Fi	Contemporary Fiction	Non-Fiction/Biography		Page number	My Rating
										☆☆☆☆☆
										☆☆☆☆☆
										☆☆☆☆☆
										☆☆☆☆☆
										☆☆☆☆☆
										☆☆☆☆☆
										☆☆☆☆☆
										☆☆☆☆☆
										☆☆☆☆☆
										☆☆☆☆☆

Book Title	Classic	Historical Fiction	Crime/Horror	Romance	Fantasy/Sci-Fi	Contemporary Fiction	Non-Fiction/Biography			Page number	My Rating
											☆☆☆☆☆
											☆☆☆☆☆
											☆☆☆☆☆
											☆☆☆☆☆
											☆☆☆☆☆
											☆☆☆☆☆
											☆☆☆☆☆
											☆☆☆☆☆
											☆☆☆☆☆
											☆☆☆☆☆

PERSONAL READING
LOG & REVIEWS

Title:_____

Author:_____Page count:_____ Genre:_____

Date started:_____Date finished:_____ Borrowed ○ Gifted ○ Own ○

Format: Audio   ○   ebook   ○   Print   ○   Other   ○

Notable moments in my life while reading:

Memorable moments in book:

Feelings this book sparked:

If I could change something about this book, it would be:

What I'll remember most:

MY THOUGHTS ABOUT
THIS BOOK

(general plot, time and place of setting, characters/people, point of view, favorite and least favorite parts, what it made me think/feel, lingering feelings after it ended, how long it took to read, overall reason for my rating)

_____

_____

_____

_____

_____

_____

_____

_____

_____

_____

_____

_____

_____

_____

_____

_____

_____

_____

Favorite quotes and lines from the book:

Who should read it:

Would I recommend this book?

Yes ◯   No ◯

My rating   ☆ ☆ ☆ ☆ ☆

Title:_____

Author:_____Page count:_____ Genre:_____

Date started:_____Date finished:_____ Borrowed ◯ Gifted ◯ Own ◯

Format: Audio   ◯   ebook   ◯   Print   ◯   Other   ◯

Notable moments in my life while reading:

Memorable moments in book:

Feelings this book sparked:

If I could change something about this book, it would be:

What I'll remember most:

MY THOUGHTS ABOUT
THIS BOOK

(general plot, time and place of setting, characters/people, point of view, favorite and least favorite parts, what it made me think/feel, lingering feelings after it ended, how long it took to read, overall reason for my rating)

_____

_____

_____

_____

_____

_____

_____

_____

_____

_____

_____

_____

_____

_____

_____

_____

_____

_____

Favorite quotes and lines from the book:

Who should read it:

Would I recommend this book?

Yes ◯   No ◯

My rating   ☆ ☆ ☆ ☆ ☆

Title:_____

Author:_____ Page count:_____ Genre:_____

Date started:_____Date finished:_____ Borrowed ○ Gifted ○ Own ○

Format: Audio ○   ebook ○   Print ○   Other ○

Notable moments in my life while reading:

Memorable moments in book:

Feelings this book sparked:

If I could change something about this book, it would be:

What I'll remember most:

MY THOUGHTS ABOUT
THIS BOOK

(general plot, time and place of setting, characters/people, point of view, favorite and least favorite parts, what it made me think/feel, lingering feelings after it ended, how long it took to read, overall reason for my rating)

_____

_____

_____

_____

_____

_____

_____

_____

_____

_____

_____

_____

_____

_____

_____

_____

_____

_____

_____

_____

Favorite quotes and lines from the book:

Who should read it:

Would I recommend this book?

Yes ○   No ○

My rating   ☆☆☆☆☆

Title:_____

Author:_____Page count:_____ Genre:_____

Date started:_____Date finished:_____ Borrowed ○ Gifted ○ Own ○

Format: Audio ○ ebook ○ Print ○ Other ○

Notable moments in my life while reading: ────────────

Memorable moments in book: ────────────

Feelings this book sparked: ────────────

If I could change something about this book, it would be: ────────────

What I'll remember most: ────────────

MY THOUGHTS ABOUT
THIS BOOK

(general plot, time and place of setting, characters/people, point of view, favorite and least favorite parts, what it made me think/feel, lingering feelings after it ended, how long it took to read, overall reason for my rating)

_____
_____
_____
_____
_____
_____
_____
_____
_____
_____
_____
_____
_____
_____
_____
_____
_____
_____

Favorite quotes and lines from the book:

Who should read it:

Would I recommend this book?

Yes ◯   No ◯

My rating   ☆☆☆☆☆

Title:_____

Author:_____Page count:_____ Genre:_____

Date started:_____Date finished:_____ Borrowed ○ Gifted ○ Own ○

Format: Audio ○ ebook ○ Print ○ Other ○

Notable moments in my life while reading:

Memorable moments in book:

Feelings this book sparked:

If I could change something about this book, it would be:

What I'll remember most:

MY THOUGHTS ABOUT
THIS BOOK

(general plot, time and place of setting, characters/people, point of view, favorite and least favorite parts, what it made me think/feel, lingering feelings after it ended, how long it took to read, overall reason for my rating)

_____

_____

_____

_____

_____

_____

_____

_____

_____

_____

_____

_____

_____

_____

_____

_____

_____

_____

Favorite quotes and lines from the book:

Who should read it:

Would I recommend this book?

Yes ◯   No ◯

My rating   ☆ ☆ ☆ ☆ ☆

Title:_____

Author:_____ Page count:_____ Genre:_____

Date started:_____Date finished:_____ Borrowed ○ Gifted ○ Own ○

Format: Audio ○   ebook ○   Print ○   Other ○

Notable moments in my life while reading:

Memorable moments in book:

Feelings this book sparked:

If I could change something about this book, it would be:

What I'll remember most:

MY THOUGHTS ABOUT
THIS BOOK

(general plot, time and place of setting, characters/people, point of view, favorite and least favorite parts, what it made me think/feel, lingering feelings after it ended, how long it took to read, overall reason for my rating)

_____
_____
_____
_____
_____
_____
_____
_____
_____
_____
_____
_____
_____
_____
_____
_____
_____
_____

Favorite quotes and lines from the book:

Who should read it:

Would I recommend this book?

Yes ○   No ○

My rating ☆ ☆ ☆ ☆ ☆

Title:_____

Author:_____Page count:_____ Genre:_____

Date started:_____Date finished:_____ Borrowed ◯ Gifted ◯ Own ◯

Format: Audio   ◯   ebook   ◯   Print   ◯   Other   ◯

Notable moments in my life while reading:

Memorable moments in book:

Feelings this book sparked:

If I could change something about this book, it would be:

What I'll remember most:

MY THOUGHTS ABOUT
THIS BOOK

(general plot, time and place of setting, characters/people, point of view, favorite and least favorite parts, what it made me think/feel, lingering feelings after it ended, how long it took to read, overall reason for my rating)

_____

_____

_____

_____

_____

_____

_____

_____

_____

_____

_____

_____

_____

_____

_____

_____

_____

_____

Favorite quotes and lines from the book:

Who should read it:

Would I recommend this book?

Yes ◯   No ◯

My rating   ☆☆☆☆☆

Title:_____

Author:_____Page count:_____ Genre:_____

Date started:_____Date finished:_____ Borrowed ○ Gifted ○ Own ○

Format: Audio   ○   ebook   ○   Print   ○   Other   ○

Notable moments in my life while reading:

Memorable moments in book:

Feelings this book sparked:

If I could change something about this book, it would be:

What I'll remember most:

MY THOUGHTS ABOUT
THIS BOOK

(general plot, time and place of setting, characters/people, point of view, favorite and least favorite parts, what it made me think/feel, lingering feelings after it ended, how long it took to read, overall reason for my rating)

_____

_____

_____

_____

_____

_____

_____

_____

_____

_____

_____

_____

_____

_____

_____

_____

_____

Favorite quotes and lines from the book:

Who should read it:

Would I recommend this book?

Yes ◯   No ◯

My rating   ☆ ☆ ☆ ☆ ☆

Title:_____

Author:_____Page count:_____ Genre:_____

Date started:_____Date finished:_____ Borrowed ◯ Gifted ◯ Own ◯

Format: Audio ◯   ebook ◯   Print ◯   Other ◯

Notable moments in my life while reading:

Memorable moments in book:

Feelings this book sparked:

If I could change something about this book, it would be:

What I'll remember most:

MY THOUGHTS ABOUT
THIS BOOK

(general plot, time and place of setting, characters/people, point of view, favorite and least favorite parts, what it made me think/feel, lingering feelings after it ended, how long it took to read, overall reason for my rating)

_____

_____

_____

_____

_____

_____

_____

_____

_____

_____

_____

_____

_____

_____

_____

_____

_____

_____

_____

Favorite quotes and lines from the book:

Who should read it:

Would I recommend this book?

Yes ◯   No ◯

My rating   ☆ ☆ ☆ ☆ ☆

Title:_____

Author:_____Page count:_____ Genre:_____

Date started:_____Date finished:_____ Borrowed ◯ Gifted ◯ Own ◯

Format: Audio ◯   ebook ◯   Print ◯   Other ◯

Notable moments in my life while reading:

Memorable moments in book:

Feelings this book sparked:

If I could change something about this book, it would be:

What I'll remember most:

MY THOUGHTS ABOUT
THIS BOOK

(general plot, time and place of setting, characters/people, point of view, favorite and least favorite parts, what it made me think/feel, lingering feelings after it ended, how long it took to read, overall reason for my rating)

_____

_____

_____

_____

_____

_____

_____

_____

_____

_____

_____

_____

_____

_____

_____

_____

_____

_____

Favorite quotes and lines from the book:

Who should read it:

Would I recommend this book?

Yes ○   No ○

My rating   ☆ ☆ ☆ ☆ ☆

Title:_____

Author:_____Page count:_____ Genre:_____

Date started:_____Date finished:_____ Borrowed ○ Gifted ○ Own ○

Format: Audio   ○   ebook   ○   Print   ○   Other   ○

Notable moments in my life while reading:

Memorable moments in book:

Feelings this book sparked:

If I could change something about this book, it would be:

What I'll remember most:

MY THOUGHTS ABOUT
THIS BOOK

(general plot, time and place of setting, characters/people, point of view, favorite and least favorite parts, what it made me think/feel, lingering feelings after it ended, how long it took to read, overall reason for my rating)

_____
_____
_____
_____
_____
_____
_____
_____
_____
_____
_____
_____
_____
_____
_____
_____
_____
_____

Favorite quotes and lines from the book:

Who should read it:

Would I recommend this book?

Yes ○   No ○

My rating   ☆ ☆ ☆ ☆ ☆

Title:_____

Author:_____ Page count:_____ Genre:_____

Date started:_____ Date finished:_____ Borrowed ◯ Gifted ◯ Own ◯

Format: Audio ◯ ebook ◯ Print ◯ Other ◯

Notable moments in my life while reading:

Memorable moments in book:

Feelings this book sparked:

If I could change something about this book, it would be:

What I'll remember most:

MY THOUGHTS ABOUT
THIS BOOK

(general plot, time and place of setting, characters/people, point of view, favorite and least favorite parts, what it made me think/feel, lingering feelings after it ended, how long it took to read, overall reason for my rating)

_____
_____
_____
_____
_____
_____
_____
_____
_____
_____
_____
_____
_____
_____
_____
_____
_____
_____
_____

Favorite quotes and lines from the book:

Who should read it:

Would I recommend this book?

Yes ◯   No ◯

My rating   ☆ ☆ ☆ ☆ ☆

Title:_____

Author:_____Page count:_____ Genre:_____

Date started:_____Date finished:_____ Borrowed ◯ Gifted ◯ Own ◯

Format: Audio   ◯   ebook   ◯   Print   ◯   Other   ◯

Notable moments in my life while reading: ───────────────

Memorable moments in book: ───────────────────────────

Feelings this book sparked: ──────────────────────────

If I could change something about this book, it would be: ──────────

What I'll remember most: ────────────────────

MY THOUGHTS ABOUT
THIS BOOK

(general plot, time and place of setting, characters/people, point of view, favorite and least favorite parts, what it made me think/feel, lingering feelings after it ended, how long it took to read, overall reason for my rating)

_____

_____

_____

_____

_____

_____

_____

_____

_____

_____

_____

_____

_____

_____

_____

_____

_____

_____

Favorite quotes and lines from the book:

Who should read it:

Would I recommend this book?

Yes ◯   No ◯

My rating   ☆ ☆ ☆ ☆ ☆

Title:_____

Author:_____Page count:_____ Genre:_____

Date started:_____Date finished:_____ Borrowed ○ Gifted ○ Own ○

Format: Audio   ○   ebook   ○   Print   ○   Other   ○

Notable moments in my life while reading:

Memorable moments in book:

Feelings this book sparked:

If I could change something about this book, it would be:

What I'll remember most:

MY THOUGHTS ABOUT
THIS BOOK

(general plot, time and place of setting, characters/people, point of view, favorite and least favorite parts, what it made me think/feel, lingering feelings after it ended, how long it took to read, overall reason for my rating)

_____

_____

_____

_____

_____

_____

_____

_____

_____

_____

_____

_____

_____

_____

_____

_____

_____

_____

_____

Favorite quotes and lines from the book:

Who should read it:

Would I recommend this book?

Yes ○   No ○

My rating ☆ ☆ ☆ ☆ ☆

Title:_____

Author:_____ Page count:_____ Genre:_____

Date started:_____Date finished:_____ Borrowed ○ Gifted ○ Own ○

Format: Audio   ○   ebook   ○   Print   ○   Other   ○

Notable moments in my life while reading:

Memorable moments in book:

Feelings this book sparked:

If I could change something about this book, it would be:

What I'll remember most:

MY THOUGHTS ABOUT
THIS BOOK

(general plot, time and place of setting, characters/people, point of view, favorite and least favorite parts, what it made me think/feel, lingering feelings after it ended, how long it took to read, overall reason for my rating)

_____

_____

_____

_____

_____

_____

_____

_____

_____

_____

_____

_____

_____

_____

_____

_____

_____

_____

Favorite quotes and lines from the book:

Who should read it:

Would I recommend this book?

Yes ◯   No ◯

My rating   ☆ ☆ ☆ ☆ ☆

Title:_____

Author:_____Page count:_____ Genre:_____

Date started:_____Date finished:_____ Borrowed ○ Gifted ○ Own ○

Format: Audio   ○   ebook   ○   Print   ○   Other   ○

Notable moments in my life while reading: ————————————————

Memorable moments in book: ————————————————————

Feelings this book sparked: ————————————————————

If I could change something about this book, it would be: ————————

What I'll remember most: ————————————————————

MY THOUGHTS ABOUT
THIS BOOK

(general plot, time and place of setting, characters/people, point of view, favorite and least favorite parts, what it made me think/feel, lingering feelings after it ended, how long it took to read, overall reason for my rating)

_____

_____

_____

_____

_____

_____

_____

_____

_____

_____

_____

_____

_____

_____

_____

_____

_____

_____

_____

Favorite quotes and lines from the book:

Who should read it:

Would I recommend this book?

Yes ◯   No ◯

My rating   ☆ ☆ ☆ ☆ ☆

Title:_____

Author:_____Page count:_____ Genre:_____

Date started:_____Date finished:_____ Borrowed ◯ Gifted ◯ Own ◯

Format: Audio   ◯   ebook   ◯   Print   ◯   Other   ◯

Notable moments in my life while reading: ——————

Memorable moments in book: ————————————————

Feelings this book sparked: ————————————————

If I could change something about this book, it would be: ——————

What I'll remember most: ————————————————

MY THOUGHTS ABOUT
THIS BOOK

(general plot, time and place of setting, characters/people, point of view, favorite and least favorite parts, what it made me think/feel, lingering feelings after it ended, how long it took to read, overall reason for my rating)

_____

_____

_____

_____

_____

_____

_____

_____

_____

_____

_____

_____

_____

_____

_____

_____

_____

_____

Favorite quotes and lines from the book:

Who should read it:

Would I recommend this book?

Yes ◯   No ◯

My rating   ☆ ☆ ☆ ☆ ☆

Title:_____

Author:_____Page count:_____ Genre:_____

Date started:_____Date finished:_____ Borrowed ○ Gifted ○ Own ○

Format: Audio ○   ebook ○   Print ○   Other ○

Notable moments in my life while reading:

Memorable moments in book:

Feelings this book sparked:

If I could change something about this book, it would be:

What I'll remember most:

MY THOUGHTS ABOUT
THIS BOOK

(general plot, time and place of setting, characters/people, point of view, favorite and least favorite parts, what it made me think/feel, lingering feelings after it ended, how long it took to read, overall reason for my rating)

_____
_____
_____
_____
_____
_____
_____
_____
_____
_____
_____
_____
_____
_____
_____
_____
_____
_____
_____

Favorite quotes and lines from the book:

Who should read it:

Would I recommend this book?

Yes ○   No ○

My rating   ☆ ☆ ☆ ☆ ☆

Title:_____

Author:_____Page count:_____ Genre:_____

Date started:_____Date finished:_____ Borrowed ○ Gifted ○ Own ○

Format: Audio   ○   ebook   ○   Print   ○   Other   ○

Notable moments in my life while reading: ─────────────

Memorable moments in book: ─────────────

Feelings this book sparked: ─────────────

If I could change something about this book, it would be: ─────────────

What I'll remember most: ─────────────

MY THOUGHTS ABOUT
THIS BOOK

(general plot, time and place of setting, characters/people, point of view, favorite and least favorite parts, what it made me think/feel, lingering feelings after it ended, how long it took to read, overall reason for my rating)

_____

_____

_____

_____

_____

_____

_____

_____

_____

_____

_____

_____

_____

_____

_____

_____

_____

_____

_____

Favorite quotes and lines from the book:

Who should read it:

Would I recommend this book?

Yes ◯   No ◯

My rating   ☆ ☆ ☆ ☆ ☆

Title:_____

Author:_____Page count:_____ Genre:_____

Date started:_____Date finished:_____ Borrowed ◯ Gifted ◯ Own ◯

Format: Audio   ◯   ebook   ◯   Print   ◯   Other   ◯

Notable moments in my life while reading:

Memorable moments in book:

Feelings this book sparked:

If I could change something about this book, it would be:

What I'll remember most:

MY THOUGHTS ABOUT
THIS BOOK

(general plot, time and place of setting, characters/people, point of view, favorite and least favorite parts, what it made me think/feel, lingering feelings after it ended, how long it took to read, overall reason for my rating)

_____
_____
_____
_____
_____
_____
_____
_____
_____
_____
_____
_____
_____
_____
_____
_____
_____
_____
_____

Favorite quotes and lines from the book:

Who should read it:

Would I recommend this book?

Yes ◯   No ◯

My rating   ☆ ☆ ☆ ☆ ☆

Title:_____

Author:_____Page count:_____ Genre:_____

Date started:_____Date finished:_____ Borrowed ○ Gifted ○ Own ○

Format: Audio ○ ebook ○ Print ○ Other ○

Notable moments in my life while reading:

Memorable moments in book:

Feelings this book sparked:

If I could change something about this book, it would be:

What I'll remember most:

MY THOUGHTS ABOUT
THIS BOOK

(general plot, time and place of setting, characters/people, point of view, favorite and least favorite parts, what it made me think/feel, lingering feelings after it ended, how long it took to read, overall reason for my rating)

_____

_____

_____

_____

_____

_____

_____

_____

_____

_____

_____

_____

_____

_____

_____

_____

_____

_____

Favorite quotes and lines from the book:

Who should read it:

Would I recommend this book?

Yes ◯   No ◯

My rating   ☆ ☆ ☆ ☆ ☆

Title:_____

Author:_____Page count:_____ Genre:_____

Date started:_____Date finished:_____ Borrowed ◯ Gifted ◯ Own ◯

Format: Audio ◯   ebook ◯   Print ◯   Other ◯

Notable moments in my life while reading:

Memorable moments in book:

Feelings this book sparked:

If I could change something about this book, it would be:

What I'll remember most:

MY THOUGHTS ABOUT
THIS BOOK

(general plot, time and place of setting, characters/people, point of view, favorite and least favorite parts, what it made me think/feel, lingering feelings after it ended, how long it took to read, overall reason for my rating)

_____

_____

_____

_____

_____

_____

_____

_____

_____

_____

_____

_____

_____

_____

_____

_____

_____

_____

_____

Favorite quotes and lines from the book:

Who should read it:

Would I recommend this book?

Yes ◯   No ◯

My rating   ☆ ☆ ☆ ☆ ☆

Title:_____

Author:_____ Page count:_____ Genre:_____

Date started:_____Date finished:_____ Borrowed ○ Gifted ○ Own ○

Format: Audio ○ ebook ○ Print ○ Other ○

Notable moments in my life while reading:

Memorable moments in book:

Feelings this book sparked:

If I could change something about this book, it would be:

What I'll remember most:

MY THOUGHTS ABOUT
THIS BOOK

(general plot, time and place of setting, characters/people, point of view, favorite and least favorite parts, what it made me think/feel, lingering feelings after it ended, how long it took to read, overall reason for my rating)

_____

_____

_____

_____

_____

_____

_____

_____

_____

_____

_____

_____

_____

_____

_____

_____

_____

_____

_____

_____

Favorite quotes and lines from the book:

Who should read it:

Would I recommend this book?

Yes ◯   No ◯

My rating   ☆☆☆☆☆

Title:_____

Author:_____Page count:_____ Genre:_____

Date started:_____Date finished:_____ Borrowed ○ Gifted ○ Own ○

Format: Audio   ○   ebook   ○   Print   ○   Other   ○

Notable moments in my life while reading:

Memorable moments in book:

Feelings this book sparked:

If I could change something about this book, it would be:

What I'll remember most:

MY THOUGHTS ABOUT
THIS BOOK

(general plot, time and place of setting, characters/people, point of view, favorite and least favorite parts, what it made me think/feel, lingering feelings after it ended, how long it took to read, overall reason for my rating)

_____

_____

_____

_____

_____

_____

_____

_____

_____

_____

_____

_____

_____

_____

_____

_____

_____

Favorite quotes and lines from the book:

Who should read it:

Would I recommend this book?

Yes ◯   No ◯

My rating   ☆☆☆☆☆

Title:_____

Author:_____Page count:_____ Genre:_____

Date started:_____Date finished:_____ Borrowed ◯ Gifted ◯ Own ◯

Format: Audio   ◯   ebook   ◯   Print   ◯   Other   ◯

Notable moments in my life while reading:

Memorable moments in book:

Feelings this book sparked:

If I could change something about this book, it would be:

What I'll remember most:

MY THOUGHTS ABOUT
THIS BOOK

(general plot, time and place of setting, characters/people, point of view, favorite and least favorite parts, what it made me think/feel, lingering feelings after it ended, how long it took to read, overall reason for my rating)

_____

_____

_____

_____

_____

_____

_____

_____

_____

_____

_____

_____

_____

_____

_____

_____

_____

_____

_____

_____

_____

Favorite quotes and lines from the book:

Who should read it:

Would I recommend this book?

Yes ◯   No ◯

My rating   ☆ ☆ ☆ ☆ ☆

Title:_____

Author:_____Page count:_____ Genre:_____

Date started:_____Date finished:_____ Borrowed ◯ Gifted ◯ Own ◯

Format: Audio   ◯   ebook   ◯   Print   ◯   Other   ◯

Notable moments in my life while reading:

Memorable moments in book:

Feelings this book sparked:

If I could change something about this book, it would be:

What I'll remember most:

MY THOUGHTS ABOUT
THIS BOOK

(general plot, time and place of setting, characters/people, point of view, favorite and least favorite parts, what it made me think/feel, lingering feelings after it ended, how long it took to read, overall reason for my rating)

_____

_____

_____

_____

_____

_____

_____

_____

_____

_____

_____

_____

_____

_____

_____

_____

_____

_____

Favorite quotes and lines from the book:

Who should read it:

Would I recommend this book?

Yes ○   No ○

My rating   ☆ ☆ ☆ ☆ ☆

Title:_____

Author:_____Page count:_____ Genre:_____

Date started:_____Date finished:_____ Borrowed ○ Gifted ○ Own ○

Format: Audio ○   ebook ○   Print ○   Other ○

Notable moments in my life while reading:

Memorable moments in book:

Feelings this book sparked:

If I could change something about this book, it would be:

What I'll remember most:

MY THOUGHTS ABOUT
THIS BOOK

(general plot, time and place of setting, characters/people, point of view, favorite and least favorite parts, what it made me think/feel, lingering feelings after it ended, how long it took to read, overall reason for my rating)

_____
_____
_____
_____
_____
_____
_____
_____
_____
_____
_____
_____
_____
_____
_____
_____
_____
_____
_____

Favorite quotes and lines from the book:

Who should read it:

Would I recommend this book?

Yes ◯   No ◯

My rating   ☆ ☆ ☆ ☆ ☆

Title:_____

Author:_____Page count:_____ Genre:_____

Date started:_____Date finished:_____ Borrowed ◯ Gifted ◯ Own ◯

Format: Audio   ◯   ebook   ◯   Print   ◯   Other   ◯

Notable moments in my life while reading:

Memorable moments in book:

Feelings this book sparked:

If I could change something about this book, it would be:

What I'll remember most:

MY THOUGHTS ABOUT
THIS BOOK

(general plot, time and place of setting, characters/people, point of view, favorite and least favorite parts, what it made me think/feel, lingering feelings after it ended, how long it took to read, overall reason for my rating)

_____

_____

_____

_____

_____

_____

_____

_____

_____

_____

_____

_____

_____

_____

_____

_____

_____

_____

Favorite quotes and lines from the book:

Who should read it:

Would I recommend this book?

Yes ○   No ○

My rating   ☆ ☆ ☆ ☆ ☆

Title:_____

Author:_____Page count:_____ Genre:_____

Date started:_____Date finished:_____ Borrowed ◯ Gifted ◯ Own ◯

Format: Audio   ◯   ebook   ◯   Print   ◯   Other   ◯

Notable moments in my life while reading:

Memorable moments in book:

Feelings this book sparked:

If I could change something about this book, it would be:

What I'll remember most:

MY THOUGHTS ABOUT
THIS BOOK

(general plot, time and place of setting, characters/people, point of view, favorite and least favorite parts, what it made me think/feel, lingering feelings after it ended, how long it took to read, overall reason for my rating)

_____

_____

_____

_____

_____

_____

_____

_____

_____

_____

_____

_____

_____

_____

_____

_____

_____

_____

Favorite quotes and lines from the book:

Who should read it:

Would I recommend this book?

Yes ◯   No ◯

My rating   ☆ ☆ ☆ ☆ ☆

Title:_____

Author:_____ Page count:_____ Genre:_____

Date started:_____Date finished:_____ Borrowed ◯ Gifted ◯ Own ◯

Format: Audio   ◯   ebook   ◯   Print   ◯   Other   ◯

Notable moments in my life while reading:

Memorable moments in book:

Feelings this book sparked:

If I could change something about this book, it would be:

What I'll remember most:

MY THOUGHTS ABOUT
THIS BOOK

(general plot, time and place of setting, characters/people, point of view, favorite and least favorite parts, what it made me think/feel, lingering feelings after it ended, how long it took to read, overall reason for my rating)

_____

_____

_____

_____

_____

_____

_____

_____

_____

_____

_____

_____

_____

_____

_____

_____

_____

_____

Favorite quotes and lines from the book:

Who should read it:

Would I recommend this book?

Yes ◯   No ◯

My rating   ☆ ☆ ☆ ☆ ☆

Title:_____

Author:_____ Page count:_____ Genre:_____

Date started:_____ Date finished:_____ Borrowed ○ Gifted ○ Own ○

Format: Audio ○   ebook ○   Print ○   Other ○

Notable moments in my life while reading: ―――――――――

Memorable moments in book: ―――――――――

Feelings this book sparked: ―――――――――

If I could change something about this book, it would be: ―――――――――

What I'll remember most: ―――――――――

MY THOUGHTS ABOUT
THIS BOOK

(general plot, time and place of setting, characters/people, point of view, favorite and least favorite parts, what it made me think/feel, lingering feelings after it
ended, how long it took to read, overall reason for my rating)

_____

_____

_____

_____

_____

_____

_____

_____

_____

_____

_____

_____

_____

_____

_____

_____

_____

_____

_____

Favorite quotes and lines from the book:

Who should read it:

Would I recommend this book?

Yes ◯   No ◯

My rating   ☆ ☆ ☆ ☆ ☆

Title:_____

Author:_____Page count:_____ Genre:_____

Date started:_____Date finished:_____ Borrowed ◯ Gifted ◯ Own ◯

Format: Audio ◯ ebook ◯ Print ◯ Other ◯

Notable moments in my life while reading:

Memorable moments in book:

Feelings this book sparked:

If I could change something about this book, it would be:

What I'll remember most:

MY THOUGHTS ABOUT
THIS BOOK

(general plot, time and place of setting, characters/people, point of view, favorite and least favorite parts, what it made me think/feel, lingering feelings after it ended, how long it took to read, overall reason for my rating)

_____

_____

_____

_____

_____

_____

_____

_____

_____

_____

_____

_____

_____

_____

_____

_____

_____

Favorite quotes and lines from the book:

Who should read it:

Would I recommend this book?

Yes ○   No ○

My rating   ☆ ☆ ☆ ☆ ☆

Title:_____

Author:_____ Page count:_____ Genre:_____

Date started:_____ Date finished:_____ Borrowed ○ Gifted ○ Own ○

Format: Audio ○ ebook ○ Print ○ Other ○

Notable moments in my life while reading:

Memorable moments in book:

Feelings this book sparked:

If I could change something about this book, it would be:

What I'll remember most:

MY THOUGHTS ABOUT
THIS BOOK

(general plot, time and place of setting, characters/people, point of view, favorite and least favorite parts, what it made me think/feel, lingering feelings after it ended, how long it took to read, overall reason for my rating)

_____

_____

_____

_____

_____

_____

_____

_____

_____

_____

_____

_____

_____

_____

_____

_____

_____

_____

_____

Favorite quotes and lines from the book:

Who should read it:

Would I recommend this book?

Yes ◯   No ◯

My rating   ☆ ☆ ☆ ☆ ☆

Title:_____

Author:_____Page count:_____ Genre:_____

Date started:_____Date finished:_____ Borrowed ○ Gifted ○ Own ○

Format: Audio ○ ebook ○ Print ○ Other ○

Notable moments in my life while reading: ─────────────

Memorable moments in book: ──────────────

Feelings this book sparked: ──────────────

If I could change something about this book, it would be: ──────

What I'll remember most: ──────────────

MY THOUGHTS ABOUT
THIS BOOK

(general plot, time and place of setting, characters/people, point of view, favorite and least favorite parts, what it made me think/feel, lingering feelings after it ended, how long it took to read, overall reason for my rating)

_____

_____

_____

_____

_____

_____

_____

_____

_____

_____

_____

_____

_____

_____

_____

_____

_____

_____

Favorite quotes and lines from the book:

Who should read it:

Would I recommend this book?

Yes ○   No ○

My rating   ☆ ☆ ☆ ☆ ☆

Title:_____

Author:_____Page count:_____ Genre:_____

Date started:_____Date finished:_____ Borrowed ◯ Gifted ◯ Own ◯

Format: Audio   ◯   ebook   ◯   Print   ◯   Other   ◯

Notable moments in my life while reading:

Memorable moments in book:

Feelings this book sparked:

If I could change something about this book, it would be:

What I'll remember most:

MY THOUGHTS ABOUT
THIS BOOK

(general plot, time and place of setting, characters/people, point of view, favorite and least favorite parts, what it made me think/feel, lingering feelings after it ended, how long it took to read, overall reason for my rating)

_____

_____

_____

_____

_____

_____

_____

_____

_____

_____

_____

_____

_____

_____

_____

_____

_____

_____

Favorite quotes and lines from the book:

Who should read it:

Would I recommend this book?

Yes ◯   No ◯

My rating   ☆ ☆ ☆ ☆ ☆

Title:_____

Author:_____Page count:_____ Genre:_____

Date started:_____Date finished:_____ Borrowed ○ Gifted ○ Own ○

Format: Audio ○   ebook ○   Print ○   Other ○

Notable moments in my life while reading:

Memorable moments in book:

Feelings this book sparked:

If I could change something about this book, it would be:

What I'll remember most:

MY THOUGHTS ABOUT
THIS BOOK

(general plot, time and place of setting, characters/people, point of view, favorite and least favorite parts, what it made me think/feel, lingering feelings after it ended, how long it took to read, overall reason for my rating)

_____

_____

_____

_____

_____

_____

_____

_____

_____

_____

_____

_____

_____

_____

_____

_____

_____

Favorite quotes and lines from the book:

Who should read it:

Would I recommend this book?

Yes ◯   No ◯

My rating   ☆ ☆ ☆ ☆ ☆

Title:_____

Author:_____Page count:_____ Genre:_____

Date started:_____Date finished:_____ Borrowed ◯ Gifted ◯ Own ◯

Format: Audio ◯   ebook ◯   Print ◯   Other ◯

Notable moments in my life while reading:

Memorable moments in book:

Feelings this book sparked:

If I could change something about this book, it would be:

What I'll remember most:

MY THOUGHTS ABOUT
THIS BOOK

(general plot, time and place of setting, characters/people, point of view, favorite and least favorite parts, what it made me think/feel, lingering feelings after it ended, how long it took to read, overall reason for my rating)

_____

_____

_____

_____

_____

_____

_____

_____

_____

_____

_____

_____

_____

_____

_____

_____

_____

Favorite quotes and lines from the book:

Who should read it:

Would I recommend this book?

Yes ◯   No ◯

My rating   ☆ ☆ ☆ ☆ ☆

Title:_____

Author:_____ Page count:_____ Genre:_____

Date started:_____ Date finished:_____ Borrowed ◯ Gifted ◯ Own ◯

Format: Audio   ◯   ebook   ◯   Print   ◯   Other   ◯

Notable moments in my life while reading:

Memorable moments in book:

Feelings this book sparked:

If I could change something about this book, it would be:

What I'll remember most:

MY THOUGHTS ABOUT
THIS BOOK

(general plot, time and place of setting, characters/people, point of view, favorite and least favorite parts, what it made me think/feel, lingering feelings after it ended, how long it took to read, overall reason for my rating)

_____

_____

_____

_____

_____

_____

_____

_____

_____

_____

_____

_____

_____

_____

_____

_____

_____

_____

Favorite quotes and lines from the book:

Who should read it:

Would I recommend this book?

Yes ○   No ○

My rating   ☆ ☆ ☆ ☆ ☆

Title:_____

Author:_____Page count:_____ Genre:_____

Date started:_____Date finished:_____ Borrowed ○ Gifted ○ Own ○

Format: Audio ○ ebook ○ Print ○ Other ○

Notable moments in my life while reading:

Memorable moments in book:

Feelings this book sparked:

If I could change something about this book, it would be:

What I'll remember most:

MY THOUGHTS ABOUT
THIS BOOK

(general plot, time and place of setting, characters/people, point of view, favorite and least favorite parts, what it made me think/feel, lingering feelings after it ended, how long it took to read, overall reason for my rating)

_____

_____

_____

_____

_____

_____

_____

_____

_____

_____

_____

_____

_____

_____

_____

_____

_____

_____

_____

Favorite quotes and lines from the book:

Who should read it:

Would I recommend this book?

Yes ◯   No ◯

My rating   ☆ ☆ ☆ ☆ ☆

Title:_____

Author:_____Page count:_____ Genre:_____

Date started:_____Date finished:_____ Borrowed ◯ Gifted ◯ Own ◯

Format: Audio   ◯   ebook   ◯   Print   ◯   Other   ◯

Notable moments in my life while reading:

Memorable moments in book:

Feelings this book sparked:

If I could change something about this book, it would be:

What I'll remember most:

MY THOUGHTS ABOUT
THIS BOOK

(general plot, time and place of setting, characters/people, point of view, favorite and least favorite parts, what it made me think/feel, lingering feelings after it ended, how long it took to read, overall reason for my rating)

_____
_____
_____
_____
_____
_____
_____
_____
_____
_____
_____
_____
_____
_____
_____
_____
_____
_____
_____
_____

Favorite quotes and lines from the book:

Who should read it:

Would I recommend this book?

Yes ◯   No ◯

My rating   ☆ ☆ ☆ ☆ ☆

Title:_____

Author:_____Page count:_____ Genre:_____

Date started:_____Date finished:_____ Borrowed ◯ Gifted ◯ Own ◯

Format: Audio ◯   ebook ◯   Print ◯   Other ◯

Notable moments in my life while reading:

Memorable moments in book:

Feelings this book sparked:

If I could change something about this book, it would be:

What I'll remember most:

MY THOUGHTS ABOUT
THIS BOOK

(general plot, time and place of setting, characters/people, point of view, favorite and least favorite parts, what it made me think/feel, lingering feelings after it ended, how long it took to read, overall reason for my rating)

_____

_____

_____

_____

_____

_____

_____

_____

_____

_____

_____

_____

_____

_____

_____

_____

_____

Favorite quotes and lines from the book:

Who should read it:

Would I recommend this book?

Yes ○   No ○

My rating   ☆ ☆ ☆ ☆ ☆

Title:_____

Author:_____ Page count:_____ Genre:_____

Date started:_____Date finished:_____ Borrowed ○ Gifted ○ Own ○

Format: Audio   ○   ebook   ○   Print   ○   Other   ○

Notable moments in my life while reading:

Memorable moments in book:

Feelings this book sparked:

If I could change something about this book, it would be:

What I'll remember most:

MY THOUGHTS ABOUT
THIS BOOK

(general plot, time and place of setting, characters/people, point of view, favorite and least favorite parts, what it made me think/feel, lingering feelings after it ended, how long it took to read, overall reason for my rating)

_____

_____

_____

_____

_____

_____

_____

_____

_____

_____

_____

_____

_____

_____

_____

_____

_____

_____

_____

Favorite quotes and lines from the book:

Who should read it:

Would I recommend this book?

Yes ◯   No ◯

My rating   ☆ ☆ ☆ ☆ ☆

Title:_____

Author:_____Page count:_____ Genre:_____

Date started:_____Date finished:_____ Borrowed ○ Gifted ○ Own ○

Format: Audio ○   ebook ○   Print ○   Other ○

Notable moments in my life while reading:

Memorable moments in book:

Feelings this book sparked:

If I could change something about this book, it would be:

What I'll remember most:

MY THOUGHTS ABOUT
THIS BOOK

(general plot, time and place of setting, characters/people, point of view, favorite and least favorite parts, what it made me think/feel, lingering feelings after it ended, how long it took to read, overall reason for my rating)

_____

_____

_____

_____

_____

_____

_____

_____

_____

_____

_____

_____

_____

_____

_____

_____

_____

_____

_____

Favorite quotes and lines from the book:

Who should read it:

Would I recommend this book?

Yes ○   No ○

My rating   ☆ ☆ ☆ ☆ ☆

Title:_____

Author:_____Page count:_____ Genre:_____

Date started:_____Date finished:_____ Borrowed ○ Gifted ○ Own ○

Format: Audio ○   ebook ○   Print ○   Other ○

Notable moments in my life while reading:

Memorable moments in book:

Feelings this book sparked:

If I could change something about this book, it would be:

What I'll remember most:

MY THOUGHTS ABOUT
THIS BOOK

(general plot, time and place of setting, characters/people, point of view, favorite and least favorite parts, what it made me think/feel, lingering feelings after it ended, how long it took to read, overall reason for my rating)

_____

_____

_____

_____

_____

_____

_____

_____

_____

_____

_____

_____

_____

_____

_____

_____

_____

_____

_____

Favorite quotes and lines from the book:

Who should read it:

Would I recommend this book?

Yes ○   No ○

My rating   ☆ ☆ ☆ ☆ ☆

Title:_____

Author:_____Page count:_____ Genre:_____

Date started:_____Date finished:_____ Borrowed ◯ Gifted ◯ Own ◯

Format:　Audio　◯　　ebook　◯　　Print　◯　　Other　◯

Notable moments in my life while reading:

Memorable moments in book:

Feelings this book sparked:

If I could change something about this book, it would be:

What I'll remember most:

MY THOUGHTS ABOUT
THIS BOOK

(general plot, time and place of setting, characters/people, point of view, favorite and least favorite parts, what it made me think/feel, lingering feelings after it ended, how long it took to read, overall reason for my rating)

_____

_____

_____

_____

_____

_____

_____

_____

_____

_____

_____

_____

_____

_____

_____

_____

_____

Favorite quotes and lines from the book:

Who should read it:

Would I recommend this book?

Yes ◯   No ◯

My rating   ☆ ☆ ☆ ☆ ☆

Title:_____

Author:_____ Page count:_____ Genre:_____

Date started:_____Date finished:_____ Borrowed ○ Gifted ○ Own ○

Format:　Audio　○　ebook　○　Print　○　Other　○

Notable moments in my life while reading: ─────────────

Memorable moments in book: ─────────────────

Feelings this book sparked: ──────────────────

If I could change something about this book, it would be: ──────

What I'll remember most: ──────────────────

MY THOUGHTS ABOUT
THIS BOOK

(general plot, time and place of setting, characters/people, point of view, favorite and least favorite parts, what it made me think/feel, lingering feelings after it ended, how long it took to read, overall reason for my rating)

_____

_____

_____

_____

_____

_____

_____

_____

_____

_____

_____

_____

_____

_____

_____

_____

_____

_____

_____

Favorite quotes and lines from the book:

Who should read it:

Would I recommend this book?

Yes ◯   No ◯

My rating   ☆ ☆ ☆ ☆ ☆

Title:_____

Author:_____Page count:_____ Genre:_____

Date started:_____Date finished:_____ Borrowed ○ Gifted ○ Own ○

Format: Audio   ○   ebook   ○   Print   ○   Other   ○

Notable moments in my life while reading: ——————————————

Memorable moments in book: ——————————————

Feelings this book sparked: ——————————————

If I could change something about this book, it would be: ——————

What I'll remember most: ——————————————

MY THOUGHTS ABOUT
THIS BOOK

(general plot, time and place of setting, characters/people, point of view, favorite and least favorite parts, what it made me think/feel, lingering feelings after it ended, how long it took to read, overall reason for my rating)

_____

_____
_____
_____
_____
_____
_____
_____
_____
_____
_____
_____
_____
_____
_____
_____
_____
_____
_____

Favorite quotes and lines from the book:

Who should read it:

Would I recommend this book?

Yes ◯   No ◯

My rating   ☆ ☆ ☆ ☆ ☆

Title:_____

Author:_____Page count:_____ Genre:_____

Date started:_____Date finished:_____ Borrowed ○ Gifted ○ Own ○

Format: Audio ○ ebook ○ Print ○ Other ○

Notable moments in my life while reading:

Memorable moments in book:

Feelings this book sparked:

If I could change something about this book, it would be:

What I'll remember most:

MY THOUGHTS ABOUT
THIS BOOK

(general plot, time and place of setting, characters/people, point of view, favorite and least favorite parts, what it made me think/feel, lingering feelings after it ended, how long it took to read, overall reason for my rating)

_____

_____

_____

_____

_____

_____

_____

_____

_____

_____

_____

_____

_____

_____

_____

_____

_____

_____

Favorite quotes and lines from the book:

Who should read it:

Would I recommend this book?

Yes ◯   No ◯

My rating   ☆ ☆ ☆ ☆ ☆

Title:_____

Author:_____Page count:_____ Genre:_____

Date started:_____Date finished:_____ Borrowed ○ Gifted ○ Own ○

Format: Audio ○   ebook ○   Print ○   Other ○

Notable moments in my life while reading: ————————

Memorable moments in book: ————————

Feelings this book sparked: ————————

If I could change something about this book, it would be: ————————

What I'll remember most: ————————

MY THOUGHTS ABOUT
THIS BOOK

(general plot, time and place of setting, characters/people, point of view, favorite and least favorite parts, what it made me think/feel, lingering feelings after it ended, how long it took to read, overall reason for my rating)

_____

_____

_____

_____

_____

_____

_____

_____

_____

_____

_____

_____

_____

_____

_____

_____

_____

Favorite quotes and lines from the book:

Who should read it:

Would I recommend this book?

Yes ◯   No ◯

My rating   ☆ ☆ ☆ ☆ ☆

Title:_____

Author:_____Page count:_____ Genre:_____

Date started:_____Date finished:_____ Borrowed ○ Gifted ○ Own ○

Format: Audio   ○   ebook   ○   Print   ○   Other   ○

Notable moments in my life while reading:

Memorable moments in book:

Feelings this book sparked:

If I could change something about this book, it would be:

What I'll remember most:

MY THOUGHTS ABOUT
THIS BOOK

(general plot, time and place of setting, characters/people, point of view, favorite and least favorite parts, what it made me think/feel, lingering feelings after it ended, how long it took to read, overall reason for my rating)

_____
_____
_____
_____
_____
_____
_____
_____
_____
_____
_____
_____
_____
_____
_____
_____
_____
_____
_____

Favorite quotes and lines from the book:

Who should read it:

Would I recommend this book?

Yes ◯   No ◯

My rating   ☆☆☆☆☆

Title:_____

Author:_____Page count:_____ Genre:_____

Date started:_____Date finished:_____ Borrowed ○ Gifted ○ Own ○

Format: Audio   ○   ebook   ○   Print   ○   Other   ○

Notable moments in my life while reading:

Memorable moments in book:

Feelings this book sparked:

If I could change something about this book, it would be:

What I'll remember most:

MY THOUGHTS ABOUT
THIS BOOK

(general plot, time and place of setting, characters/people, point of view, favorite and least favorite parts, what it made me think/feel, lingering feelings after it ended, how long it took to read, overall reason for my rating)

_____

_____

_____

_____

_____

_____

_____

_____

_____

_____

_____

_____

_____

_____

_____

_____

_____

_____

_____

Favorite quotes and lines from the book:

Who should read it:

Would I recommend this book?

Yes ◯   No ◯

My rating   ☆ ☆ ☆ ☆ ☆

Title:_____

Author:_____Page count:_____ Genre:_____

Date started:_____Date finished:_____ Borrowed ◯ Gifted ◯ Own ◯

Format: Audio ◯ ebook ◯ Print ◯ Other ◯

Notable moments in my life while reading:

Memorable moments in book:

Feelings this book sparked:

If I could change something about this book, it would be:

What I'll remember most:

MY THOUGHTS ABOUT
THIS BOOK

(general plot, time and place of setting, characters/people, point of view, favorite and least favorite parts, what it made me think/feel, lingering feelings after it ended, how long it took to read, overall reason for my rating)

_____
_____
_____
_____
_____
_____
_____
_____
_____
_____
_____
_____
_____
_____
_____
_____
_____
_____

Favorite quotes and lines from the book:

Who should read it:

Would I recommend this book?

Yes ◯   No ◯

My rating ☆ ☆ ☆ ☆ ☆

Title:_____

Author:_____Page count:_____ Genre:_____

Date started:_____Date finished:_____ Borrowed ◯ Gifted ◯ Own ◯

Format: Audio   ◯   ebook   ◯   Print   ◯   Other   ◯

Notable moments in my life while reading:

Memorable moments in book:

Feelings this book sparked:

If I could change something about this book, it would be:

What I'll remember most:

MY THOUGHTS ABOUT
THIS BOOK

(general plot, time and place of setting, characters/people, point of view, favorite and least favorite parts, what it made me think/feel, lingering feelings after it ended, how long it took to read, overall reason for my rating)

_____

_____

_____

_____

_____

_____

_____

_____

_____

_____

_____

_____

_____

_____

_____

_____

_____

_____

_____

Favorite quotes and lines from the book:

Who should read it:

Would I recommend this book?

Yes ○   No ○

My rating   ☆ ☆ ☆ ☆ ☆

Title:_____

Author:_____Page count:_____ Genre:_____

Date started:_____Date finished:_____ Borrowed ○ Gifted ○ Own ○

Format: Audio ○   ebook ○   Print ○   Other ○

Notable moments in my life while reading:

Memorable moments in book:

Feelings this book sparked:

If I could change something about this book, it would be:

What I'll remember most:

MY THOUGHTS ABOUT
THIS BOOK

(general plot, time and place of setting, characters/people, point of view, favorite and least favorite parts, what it made me think/feel, lingering feelings after it ended, how long it took to read, overall reason for my rating)

_____

_____

_____

_____

_____

_____

_____

_____

_____

_____

_____

_____

_____

_____

_____

_____

_____

_____

_____

Favorite quotes and lines from the book:

Who should read it:

Would I recommend this book?

Yes ○　　　No ○

My rating ☆☆☆☆☆

Title:_____

Author:_____Page count:_____ Genre:_____

Date started:_____Date finished:_____ Borrowed ○ Gifted ○ Own ○

Format: Audio ○   ebook ○   Print ○   Other ○

Notable moments in my life while reading: ——————————

Memorable moments in book: ——————————

Feelings this book sparked: ——————————

If I could change something about this book, it would be: ——————————

What I'll remember most: ——————————

MY THOUGHTS ABOUT
THIS BOOK

(general plot, time and place of setting, characters/people, point of view, favorite and least favorite parts, what it made me think/feel, lingering feelings after it ended, how long it took to read, overall reason for my rating)

_____

_____

_____

_____

_____

_____

_____

_____

_____

_____

_____

_____

_____

_____

_____

_____

_____

_____

_____

Favorite quotes and lines from the book:

Who should read it:

Would I recommend this book?

Yes ◯   No ◯

My rating   ☆ ☆ ☆ ☆ ☆

Title:_____

Author:_____Page count:_____ Genre:_____

Date started:_____Date finished:_____ Borrowed ○ Gifted ○ Own ○

Format: Audio   ○   ebook   ○   Print   ○   Other   ○

Notable moments in my life while reading: ─────────

Memorable moments in book: ─────────

Feelings this book sparked: ─────────

If I could change something about this book, it would be: ─────────

What I'll remember most: ─────────

MY THOUGHTS ABOUT
THIS BOOK

(general plot, time and place of setting, characters/people, point of view, favorite and least favorite parts, what it made me think/feel, lingering feelings after it ended, how long it took to read, overall reason for my rating)

_____

_____

_____

_____

_____

_____

_____

_____

_____

_____

_____

_____

_____

_____

_____

_____

_____

_____

Favorite quotes and lines from the book:

Who should read it:

Would I recommend this book?

Yes ◯   No ◯

My rating   ☆ ☆ ☆ ☆ ☆

Title:_____

Author:_____ Page count:_____ Genre:_____

Date started:_____Date finished:_____ Borrowed ○ Gifted ○ Own ○

Format: Audio ○ ebook ○ Print ○ Other ○

Notable moments in my life while reading: ─────────────

Memorable moments in book: ─────────────

Feelings this book sparked: ─────────────

If I could change something about this book, it would be: ─────────────

What I'll remember most: ─────────────

MY THOUGHTS ABOUT
THIS BOOK

(general plot, time and place of setting, characters/people, point of view, favorite and least favorite parts, what it made me think/feel, lingering feelings after it ended, how long it took to read, overall reason for my rating)

_____

_____

_____

_____

_____

_____

_____

_____

_____

_____

_____

_____

_____

_____

_____

_____

_____

_____

_____

_____

_____

Favorite quotes and lines from the book:

Who should read it:

Would I recommend this book?

Yes ◯   No ◯

My rating   ☆ ☆ ☆ ☆ ☆

Title:_____

Author:_____Page count:_____ Genre:_____

Date started:_____Date finished:_____ Borrowed ◯ Gifted ◯ Own ◯

Format: Audio ◯ ebook ◯ Print ◯ Other ◯

Notable moments in my life while reading: ————————————————

Memorable moments in book: ————————————————

Feelings this book sparked: ————————————————

If I could change something about this book, it would be: ————————————

What I'll remember most: ————————————————

MY THOUGHTS ABOUT
THIS BOOK

(general plot, time and place of setting, characters/people, point of view, favorite and least favorite parts, what it made me think/feel, lingering feelings after it ended, how long it took to read, overall reason for my rating)

_____

_____

_____

_____

_____

_____

_____

_____

_____

_____

_____

_____

_____

_____

_____

_____

_____

_____

_____

Favorite quotes and lines from the book:

Who should read it:

Would I recommend this book?

Yes ◯   No ◯

My rating   ☆ ☆ ☆ ☆ ☆

Title:_____

Author:_____Page count:_____ Genre:_____

Date started:_____Date finished:_____ Borrowed ◯ Gifted ◯ Own ◯

Format: Audio   ◯   ebook   ◯   Print   ◯   Other   ◯

Notable moments in my life while reading:

Memorable moments in book:

Feelings this book sparked:

If I could change something about this book, it would be:

What I'll remember most:

MY THOUGHTS ABOUT
THIS BOOK

(general plot, time and place of setting, characters/people, point of view, favorite and least favorite parts, what it made me think/feel, lingering feelings after it ended, how long it took to read, overall reason for my rating)

_____

_____

_____

_____

_____

_____

_____

_____

_____

_____

_____

_____

_____

_____

_____

_____

_____

_____

Favorite quotes and lines from the book:

Who should read it:

Would I recommend this book?

Yes ◯   No ◯

My rating   ☆ ☆ ☆ ☆ ☆

Title:_____

Author:_____ Page count:_____ Genre:_____

Date started:_____ Date finished:_____ Borrowed ◯ Gifted ◯ Own ◯

Format: Audio   ◯   ebook   ◯   Print   ◯   Other   ◯

Notable moments in my life while reading: ———————————————

Memorable moments in book: ————————————————————

Feelings this book sparked: ————————————————————

If I could change something about this book, it would be: ——————

What I'll remember most: ——————————————————————

MY THOUGHTS ABOUT
THIS BOOK

(general plot, time and place of setting, characters/people, point of view, favorite and least favorite parts, what it made me think/feel, lingering feelings after it ended, how long it took to read, overall reason for my rating)

_____

_____

_____

_____

_____

_____

_____

_____

_____

_____

_____

_____

_____

_____

_____

_____

_____

_____

_____

Favorite quotes and lines from the book:

Who should read it:

Would I recommend this book?

Yes ◯   No ◯

My rating   ☆ ☆ ☆ ☆ ☆

Title:_____

Author:_____ Page count:_____ Genre:_____

Date started:_____Date finished:_____ Borrowed ◯ Gifted ◯ Own ◯

Format: Audio ◯ ebook ◯ Print ◯ Other ◯

Notable moments in my life while reading: ——————————

Memorable moments in book: ——————————

Feelings this book sparked: ——————————

If I could change something about this book, it would be: ——————————

What I'll remember most: ——————————

MY THOUGHTS ABOUT
THIS BOOK

(general plot, time and place of setting, characters/people, point of view, favorite and least favorite parts, what it made me think/feel, lingering feelings after it ended, how long it took to read, overall reason for my rating)

_____

_____

_____

_____

_____

_____

_____

_____

_____

_____

_____

_____

_____

_____

_____

_____

_____

_____

Favorite quotes and lines from the book:

Who should read it:

Would I recommend this book?

Yes ◯   No ◯

My rating   ☆ ☆ ☆ ☆ ☆

Title:_____

Author:_____Page count:_____ Genre:_____

Date started:_____Date finished:_____ Borrowed ○ Gifted ○ Own ○

Format: Audio   ○   ebook   ○   Print   ○   Other   ○

Notable moments in my life while reading:

Memorable moments in book:

Feelings this book sparked:

If I could change something about this book, it would be:

What I'll remember most:

MY THOUGHTS ABOUT
THIS BOOK

(general plot, time and place of setting, characters/people, point of view, favorite and least favorite parts, what it made me think/feel, lingering feelings after it ended, how long it took to read, overall reason for my rating)

_____

_____

_____

_____

_____

_____

_____

_____

_____

_____

_____

_____

_____

_____

_____

_____

_____

_____

Favorite quotes and lines from the book:

Who should read it:

Would I recommend this book?

Yes ◯   No ◯

My rating   ☆ ☆ ☆ ☆ ☆

Title:_____

Author:_____Page count:_____ Genre:_____

Date started:_____Date finished:_____ Borrowed ○ Gifted ○ Own ○

Format: Audio ○ ebook ○ Print ○ Other ○

Notable moments in my life while reading:

Memorable moments in book:

Feelings this book sparked:

If I could change something about this book, it would be:

What I'll remember most:

MY THOUGHTS ABOUT
THIS BOOK

(general plot, time and place of setting, characters/people, point of view, favorite and least favorite parts, what it made me think/feel, lingering feelings after it ended, how long it took to read, overall reason for my rating)

_____

_____

_____

_____

_____

_____

_____

_____

_____

_____

_____

_____

_____

_____

_____

_____

_____

_____

_____

Favorite quotes and lines from the book:

Who should read it:

Would I recommend this book?

Yes ◯   No ◯

My rating ☆☆☆☆☆

Title:_____

Author:_____Page count:_____ Genre:_____

Date started:_____Date finished:_____ Borrowed ○ Gifted ○ Own ○

Format: Audio ○   ebook ○   Print ○   Other ○

Notable moments in my life while reading:

Memorable moments in book:

Feelings this book sparked:

If I could change something about this book, it would be:

What I'll remember most:

MY THOUGHTS ABOUT
THIS BOOK

(general plot, time and place of setting, characters/people, point of view, favorite and least favorite parts, what it made me think/feel, lingering feelings after it ended, how long it took to read, overall reason for my rating)

_____
_____
_____
_____
_____
_____
_____
_____
_____
_____
_____
_____
_____
_____
_____
_____
_____
_____
_____

Favorite quotes and lines from the book:

Who should read it:

Would I recommend this book?

Yes ◯   No ◯

My rating ☆☆☆☆☆

Title:_____

Author:_____Page count:_____ Genre:_____

Date started:_____Date finished:_____ Borrowed ○ Gifted ○ Own ○

Format: Audio   ○   ebook   ○   Print   ○   Other   ○

Notable moments in my life while reading: ———————

Memorable moments in book: ———————————

Feelings this book sparked: ————————————

If I could change something about this book, it would be: ———

What I'll remember most: ————————————

MY THOUGHTS ABOUT
THIS BOOK

(general plot, time and place of setting, characters/people, point of view, favorite and least favorite parts, what it made me think/feel, lingering feelings after it ended, how long it took to read, overall reason for my rating)

_____
_____
_____
_____
_____
_____
_____
_____
_____
_____
_____
_____
_____
_____
_____
_____
_____
_____
_____

Favorite quotes and lines from the book:

Who should read it:

Would I recommend this book?

Yes ◯   No ◯

My rating   ☆ ☆ ☆ ☆ ☆

Title:_____

Author:_____Page count:_____ Genre:_____

Date started:_____Date finished:_____ Borrowed ○ Gifted ○ Own ○

Format: Audio   ○   ebook   ○   Print   ○   Other   ○

Notable moments in my life while reading: ——————————

Memorable moments in book: ——————————

Feelings this book sparked: ——————————

If I could change something about this book, it would be: ——————————

What I'll remember most: ——————————

MY THOUGHTS ABOUT
THIS BOOK

(general plot, time and place of setting, characters/people, point of view, favorite and least favorite parts, what it made me think/feel, lingering feelings after it ended, how long it took to read, overall reason for my rating)

_____
_____
_____
_____
_____
_____
_____
_____
_____
_____
_____
_____
_____
_____
_____
_____
_____
_____

Favorite quotes and lines from the book:

Who should read it:

Would I recommend this book?

Yes ◯   No ◯

My rating   ☆☆☆☆☆

Title:_____

Author:_____Page count:_____ Genre:_____

Date started:_____Date finished:_____ Borrowed ◯ Gifted ◯ Own ◯

Format: Audio ◯   ebook ◯   Print ◯   Other ◯

Notable moments in my life while reading:

Memorable moments in book:

Feelings this book sparked:

If I could change something about this book, it would be:

What I'll remember most:

MY THOUGHTS ABOUT
THIS BOOK

(general plot, time and place of setting, characters/people, point of view, favorite and least favorite parts, what it made me think/feel, lingering feelings after it ended, how long it took to read, overall reason for my rating)

_____

_____

_____

_____

_____

_____

_____

_____

_____

_____

_____

_____

_____

_____

_____

_____

_____

_____

Favorite quotes and lines from the book:

Who should read it:

Would I recommend this book?

Yes ○   No ○

My rating   ☆ ☆ ☆ ☆ ☆

ADDITIONAL NOTES

BOOK CLUB
DISCUSSION GUIDE

BOOK CLUB DISCUSSION GUIDE

- What was your favorite part of this book?

- What was your least favorite part of this book?

- What characters or people stood out to you?

- Did anything surprise you about this book?

- What did this book reveal to you about yourself?

- How long did it take to read this book? Why do you think you went so quickly or slowly?

- Which feelings did this book bring up? What parts (or characters) elicited these feelings?

- What was most memorable about this book?

- Did you have any favorite passages or quotes from this book?

BOOK CLUB DISCUSSION GUIDE

- Was this book underrated, worth the hype, or just as expected?

- If this book were a movie, who would be cast?

- If someone were to judge this book by its cover, what would they think?

- If you were to recommend songs to go with the reading of this book, what would they be?

- Are you interested in reading other books by this author? Why or why not?

- What do you think the author of this book wanted you to know?

- If you had to summarize this book with only one word, what word would that be?

- What aspects of this story could you most relate to?

- What questions still lingered for you at the end of this book?

BOOK CLUB DISCUSSION GUIDE

Fiction Only:

- If you could change one thing about this story, what would it be?

- If you could meet one of the characters in real life, which one would you choose and why?

- If you could have chosen an alternative ending, what would it be?

Nonfiction Only:

- What did you already know about the topic of this book? If already familiar, how did your perspective change while reading?

- Did you look up anything about the subject matter while reading?

- How might the world be different if the people in this book had made different choices, or if the events in this book had not taken place at all?

BOOKS
TO READ

BOOKS TO READ

Title:_____ Author:_____
Why it's on my list:_____

Title:_____ Author:_____
Why it's on my list:_____

Title:_____ Author:_____
Why it's on my list:_____

Title:_____ Author:_____
Why it's on my list:_____

Title:_____ Author:_____
Why it's on my list:_____

Title:_____ Author:_____
Why it's on my list:_____

Title:_____ Author:_____
Why it's on my list:_____

Title:_____ Author:_____
Why it's on my list:_____

Title:_____ Author:_____
Why it's on my list:_____

Title:_____ Author:_____
Why it's on my list:_____

Title:_____ Author:_____
Why it's on my list:_____

BOOKS TO READ

Title:_____ Author:_____
Why it's on my list:_____

Title:_____ Author:_____
Why it's on my list:_____

Title:_____ Author:_____
Why it's on my list:_____

Title:_____ Author:_____
Why it's on my list:_____

Title:_____ Author:_____
Why it's on my list:_____

Title:_____ Author:_____
Why it's on my list:_____

Title:_____ Author:_____
Why it's on my list:_____

Title:_____ Author:_____
Why it's on my list:_____

Title:_____ Author:_____
Why it's on my list:_____

Title:_____ Author:_____
Why it's on my list:_____

Title:_____ Author:_____
Why it's on my list:_____

BOOKS TO READ

Title:_____ Author:_____
Why it's on my list:_____

Title:_____ Author:_____
Why it's on my list:_____

Title:_____ Author:_____
Why it's on my list:_____

Title:_____ Author:_____
Why it's on my list:_____

Title:_____ Author:_____
Why it's on my list:_____

Title:_____ Author:_____
Why it's on my list:_____

Title:_____ Author:_____
Why it's on my list:_____

Title:_____ Author:_____
Why it's on my list:_____

Title:_____ Author:_____
Why it's on my list:_____

Title:_____ Author:_____
Why it's on my list:_____

Title:_____ Author:_____
Why it's on my list:_____

Title:_____ Author:_____
Why it's on my list:_____

FRIEND LENDING
LIBRARY

FRIEND LENDING LIBRARY

Book title:	Borrowed from/lent to:	Date borrowed:	Date returned:

FRIEND LENDING LIBRARY

Book title:	Borrowed from/lent to:	Date borrowed:	Date returned:

FRIEND LENDING LIBRARY

Book title:	Borrowed from/lent to:	Date borrowed:	Date returned:

THEY SHOULD
READ THIS

THEY SHOULD READ THIS

Book title:	Who should read it:	Why:

THEY SHOULD READ THIS

Book title:	Who should read it:	Why:

THEY SHOULD READ THIS

Book title:	Who should read it:	Why:

READING
HABITS CALENDAR

READING HABITS CALENDAR

How many books read in_____
year

Jan	Feb	Mar	Apr	May	Jun	Jul	Aug	Sep	Oct	Nov	Dec
○	○	○	○	○	○	○	○	○	○	○	○
○	○	○	○	○	○	○	○	○	○	○	○
○	○	○	○	○	○	○	○	○	○	○	○
○	○	○	○	○	○	○	○	○	○	○	○
○	○	○	○	○	○	○	○	○	○	○	○
○	○	○	○	○	○	○	○	○	○	○	○
○	○	○	○	○	○	○	○	○	○	○	○
○	○	○	○	○	○	○	○	○	○	○	○
○	○	○	○	○	○	○	○	○	○	○	○
○	○	○	○	○	○	○	○	○	○	○	○
○	○	○	○	○	○	○	○	○	○	○	○

How many books read in_____
year

Jan	Feb	Mar	Apr	May	Jun	Jul	Aug	Sep	Oct	Nov	Dec
○	○	○	○	○	○	○	○	○	○	○	○
○	○	○	○	○	○	○	○	○	○	○	○
○	○	○	○	○	○	○	○	○	○	○	○
○	○	○	○	○	○	○	○	○	○	○	○
○	○	○	○	○	○	○	○	○	○	○	○
○	○	○	○	○	○	○	○	○	○	○	○
○	○	○	○	○	○	○	○	○	○	○	○
○	○	○	○	○	○	○	○	○	○	○	○
○	○	○	○	○	○	○	○	○	○	○	○
○	○	○	○	○	○	○	○	○	○	○	○
○	○	○	○	○	○	○	○	○	○	○	○

READING HABITS CALENDAR

How many books read in_____
                              year

Jan	Feb	Mar	Apr	May	Jun	Jul	Aug	Sep	Oct	Nov	Dec
○	○	○	○	○	○	○	○	○	○	○	○
○	○	○	○	○	○	○	○	○	○	○	○
○	○	○	○	○	○	○	○	○	○	○	○
○	○	○	○	○	○	○	○	○	○	○	○
○	○	○	○	○	○	○	○	○	○	○	○
○	○	○	○	○	○	○	○	○	○	○	○
○	○	○	○	○	○	○	○	○	○	○	○
○	○	○	○	○	○	○	○	○	○	○	○
○	○	○	○	○	○	○	○	○	○	○	○
○	○	○	○	○	○	○	○	○	○	○	○
○	○	○	○	○	○	○	○	○	○	○	○

How many books read in_____
                              year

Jan	Feb	Mar	Apr	May	Jun	Jul	Aug	Sep	Oct	Nov	Dec
○	○	○	○	○	○	○	○	○	○	○	○
○	○	○	○	○	○	○	○	○	○	○	○
○	○	○	○	○	○	○	○	○	○	○	○
○	○	○	○	○	○	○	○	○	○	○	○
○	○	○	○	○	○	○	○	○	○	○	○
○	○	○	○	○	○	○	○	○	○	○	○
○	○	○	○	○	○	○	○	○	○	○	○
○	○	○	○	○	○	○	○	○	○	○	○
○	○	○	○	○	○	○	○	○	○	○	○
○	○	○	○	○	○	○	○	○	○	○	○
○	○	○	○	○	○	○	○	○	○	○	○

ABOUT THE AUTHOR

Melissa Pennel is a mother, life coach, and author. She believes that books tell us the story of ourselves, that everyone is a writer if given the right prompts, and that every life (and story) matters. Melissa lives in Northern California with her partner, children, and beloved cats.

Find more of Melissa's work at FollowYourFireCoaching.com

www.ingramcontent.com/pod-product-compliance
Lightning Source LLC
Chambersburg PA
CBHW022055020426
42335CB00012B/699